Discovery
Moon Phases

By Jayna A'Janee Smith

Cover Art By kiki Elice
@kiki_elice

Contents
***

Foreword
***

"He's written about a new moon, Hilal. Now he'll write about the full moon, the sheikh. New moon and full moon are the same. A new moon teaches gradualness and deliberation, and how one gives birth to oneself slowly. Patience with small details makes perfect a large work, like the universe. What nine months of attention does for an embryo, forty early mornings will do for your gradually growing wholeness." – Rumi

The Seasons:
    Fall
        Winter

            Spring
                Summer

The Senses:
    Seeing
        Hearing
          Smelling
            Tasting
              Touching

In her book of poetry Ms. Jayna A'janee Smith has linked, or connected the reader's seasons of life to stimulate our senses. We need a shield of silence in order to focus on things that are uneven. The downfall of our modern day environment is the overstimulation of our seasons and our senses, which delays our movement toward a more humane world. Rumi and Ms. Smith offer us a way forward.

From My Heart
*****

This book was written in stages. Over so many difficult, confusing, devastating, numb, enlightening phases. These poems are snapshots of some of the most impactful experiences—pieces of moments that once puzzled my mind. Ponderings of the leftover pieces I still can't seem to fit into the right place in my heart. I can't begin to describe how much of myself I had to bend and stretch to put pen to paper, hands to keys in the moments that paralyzed me. So many experiences in my life have contributed to this collection of life lessons. This is the journey of womanhood, a story of pain and healing.

I needed this book as much as you do, but we are on the other side of writing it now, and I'm sharing it with you, because you need it. You need to know you aren't alone in these feelings, emotions and truths. You need to know that you aren't alone in choosing to love someone else before you learned to love yourself. You need to know that there's no such thing as perfect beginnings and endings, but life is about everything in between. You need to know that in pain there is healing, and in healing there is pain. I realize that I will be discovering new truths my whole life. This season has truly been one of ongoing discovery, and one of the most significant discoveries I have made is that sharing truths is healing. It's just as healing for the person sharing, as those on the other end. I hope you *discover* yourself as you take a journey through my "Moon Phases."

*Dedicated to my nephew Pradis Amen Andrews III
and the baby I lost while still in my womb*
Forever in My Heart
♥ ♥ ♥ ♥

WAXING CRESCENT MOON

There were parts of her hidden and unseen
*****

<u>Rainbow</u>

when raindrops slow,
and the sun breaks through the clouds
tears slowly subside.

the rainbow
only appears
when the sun
battles the clouds.

to love self through pain

Garden

whispers
often carry
unsolicited
advice
from
pursed lips and
"rapey eyes"
young girl
your value
lies
in the
blooming rose
between
your legs,
your
stock
drops
every time you
open your legs…

woman
your rose is   withering

your   seed

is already more valuable than you

forget that
while your   vagina is
a   single   flower

your mind is a

beautiful garden

9

Resentment

you weren't wearing cologne,
but your scent still lingers.
i get whiffs of you
and it reminds me of dead flowers.

i don't want to remember you,
but your name sits on my tongue
like the remnants of a bitter fruit

i don't want to remember you,
but when i think of
red watermelon,
pink sweats,
or your ugly brown house
i tell myself i can't...

i can't risk forgetting how much i hate you.
for being a horrible memory that lingers.
for being the one who stole my innocence

Two Sides to the Story

leftover scars
told misleading
tales of things that
happened to me,
i tattooed over
them—
i own the rights
to my story

not a victim

Sympathy

as you purse your lips
to speak
my stomach turns,
i know that
look on your face
and today
kindness hurts

<u>Siphoned</u>

it got to a critical
point before
i realized
full-filling you
was draining me

i deserve to be refilled too

Dump

you have always
dumped on me
like i was a waste yard
for all of your
bad energy
i was a fool to accept
what i couldn't
recycle,
expecting that your
trash
could ever be
another's treasure

Heavy

she was heavy enough to sink
in the Dead Sea,
and under all that pressure
it perplexed me
how she could have ever
walked with her head up,
or opened her mouth.
and you wonder why
she didn't ask for help.
she wanted to float.
to experience the healing nutrients
the salt would deposit,
but her jaws were locked
under the weight
of her sadness

Runaway Horse

like the back of a stallion
there is a
heavy burden
for the
passionate
to be strong enough to carry
to be strong enough to stay

for my brother

Lost

running from pain
i hid myself
until
so little was left
i couldn't
identify
with many of the
words i thought
or said

they were lies

Abandoned

comfort should
never come
in knowing
you love me,
but will
never call

Enough

every time
you say
you're trying
i wonder…
if the roles
were reversed
would your
effort be enough?

Absent

it's disappointing
to call your name
knowing dead air
will fill the space
your presence should
exist in.

you're going to miss
what's left of your life
trying to make up for
unexcused absences.

you'd rather live in the past,
or spend now thinking about the future,
and none of that will
reconcile the time you've wasted.

you really don't get
that you being _here_
is the only real present

to my dear parents

Scapegoat

look at the wounds
      i've sustained
falling on your sword

will you ever
take responsibility?

looking for forgiveness
for your indiscretions
like i was your savior

i won't keep offering
understanding
when my feelings
are never a thought

i've already sacrificed a lot

Bittersweet

you kiss
my scars,
as if that erases
how they got there
in the first place

<u>Missing Pieces</u>

i sacrificed valuable
parts of me
to keep you
whole
when you just wanted
to be broken

Mosaic

forgive me
for not accepting
your truth,
forgive me
for not seeing
you're
Mmmmmmmmmmmm
Ooooooooooooooooooo
Sssssssssssssssssssssssss
Aaaaaaaaaaaaaaaaaaaaa
Iiiiiiiiiiiiiiiiiiiiiiiiiiiiiiiiiiiiiiiiiii
Cccccccccccccccccccccccc

Help

they say just ask.
but what happens
when i
SCREAM
and no sound
reverberates?
or when i cry
and not one
tear dampens
my face?
how do i ask for
HELP
when i don't even know
i need it

Lifeboat

what was a lifeboat
during tragedy,
may no longer serve you
once you remove
the calamity

Selfish

you have always been
my weakness,
so my strength
grows with distance

these boundaries
are for me.

i'll stop calling you selfish
when my healing
is no longer perceived
as an attack on you

Exchange

you told me it's
all or nothing
with you
but,
i'm tired of
giving
all of me
in exchange for
parts of you

<u>*Worry*</u>

living with anxiety
is like trying to
capture and hold
rushing water
hands pressed
together tightly—
fingers laced

i'm anxious thinking
about all the water—all the life
i waste

Flowers & Weeds

i planted
orchid seeds
in our garden
of love,
but your lies
sprouted weeds
that tainted the soil,
you poisoned the
chance of
us ever growing
anything beautiful

Invaluable

you were here
to relish
the diamonds
and rubies that flow
from my mouth

others came
to tap
oil that flows
from the wells
between my legs

the difference between a native and a colonizer

Potent-ial

you said your
love was potent,
when you called
yourself
falling for
potent-ial

i loved you
flaws and all
not for who
you'd be in the future

Lying Lips

sometimes i stare
at your lips
and wonder how
they could be
so ambivalent,

when they're closed
gently pressed against mine
i swear i hear them saying
you love me,

but when you
open them
in anger,
i know that
can't be

Honey

you could have
liquid gold honey,
but you keep settling
for artificial sweetener

Forbidden Fruit

we bathed in the fruits
of each other's sins.
your sweet lips
drip of agave lime,
mine carry a scent of
royal purple,
cloaked over fiery green

poisons coursing through
our veins like chemo,
we didn't choose it
we were already sick.
infected at conception.

i don't run from what
i am
i just numb it,
don't always like
who i am,
but i own it

when i'm lost in you,
and you're lost in me.
we find fragments
of ourselves in one another
praying that as we share
we don't bring hell
to one another.

i'd be lying
if i said it doesn't
feel good
to share these fruits
with another

your friendship is enabling

Silence

i suffocated on
words unspoken
for too long
to watch you waste
precious energy
not speaking to me

Quiet Storm

you told me you
erected walls
to keep people out

you didn't tell me
it was to save them
from your wake.

i found myself,
staring into the eye of
the storm

you can't keep
me trapped
i'll drown in your
maelstrom

Ego

i'm done stretching myself
to fit into a space
overrun with your ego
i've never been small,
but in your eyes
i've never been big enough

you don't see me

Love Language

you were disappointed
when we didn't work,
but not enough
to change
you have to understand—
it was your choice
to love me,
you don't get to
choose what way

Misguided Affection

forgive me.
i must've confused
being in love,
with knowing you
deserve to be

<u>*Star*</u>

eyes as numerous as the stars
have shined on me
but only two have witnessed
the wonder of my soliloquy
even if we only shared
a momentary glance
it was transformative to speak
and watch
as your eyes danced

-the first time someone saw me

Favorite blanket

i was cold
and there you were
all warm and cozy
snuggled up on the shelf.
i was tired of being
alone-— freezing
and i just wanted
a blanket.
to wrap around
my frame.
to hug me.
to rest.
gently on my bare skin
so i chose you.
it didn't matter
that you weren't
a hand woven tapestry,
or a geometric
patterned duvet.
while i was cold
you were everything
i needed and more,

but what was to become
of my once favorite blanket?
when the winter passed
and the sun now
warmed me.
would i fold you up and store
you away for a rainy day?
would i gift you to the next person
who stood teeth chattering?
would it be easy
to remember the chill
of the cold air, or would i grow

too comfortable with you?

and take for granted
all that a simple blanket
provided all the times
i was cold.

Double-edged-sword

the double-edged sword
you pulled out my back
sliced through your fingers
and somehow I
found time to empathize
like what was hurting you
wasn't also killing me

<u>*Grapefruit*</u>

cloaked in
complexity
i was the sweetest
ruby red,
you opted for
simplicity
and settled for bitter
hanging fruit
instead

Scorched

starring in your eyes is like the time
i scorched my own gazing at the sun.
i knew i shouldn't.
but i was amazed,
and believed finally seeing you
was well worth the burn.

Anchor

i don't want to be
chained to you anymore,
and not for
the reasons you think
i feel myself
s
i
n
k
i
n
g
there's a
h-o-l-e- in my vest,
my job has always been
to hold you down
but i can't.
with the weight of the world
c
      r
  a
   s
h
   i
n
     g
down on me.
i don't want to be your anchor
when you're trying to swim.

NEW MOON

There were faces all claiming her name. None of them were hers.
*****

Blacker The Berry

no one ever told me
to grow wild
like a blackberry.
to ripen.
to sweeten.
to bloom.
no one ever taught me
how to grow unrestrained.
to occupy space without condition.
to be the blackest and sweetest berry,
to be the one that isn't picked.
no one ever taught me
how to grow.

Fire & Ice

she was hard…

hard to touch
hard of hearing
hardly easy to love—
above the surface

        she was ice

        she was light…

        warm to touch
        warm in speech
        warmly intimate—
        below the surface

                she was fire

Bound No More

i can't keep
granting you
unlimited access...

healthy boundaries
aren't the
antithesis of love,
they are the
prerequisite

Water

the best gift i ever received
was a small plant
with a note attached
water and sing.
every day i poured into it.
and every day
it exhaled oxygen

<u>Whole</u>

you tied
yourself to
many
before you
realized
you were
already whole

Mother of the Earth

naked eve
in shame
cloaked herself
in figs and leaves.
the mother of mothers
clipped her wings,
walked
through gardens
into winter storms
unable to withstand
elements once
manipulated by her form
the turn of her hand
the sway of her hips,
instead of passing on
her gifts
she gave birth to daughters
who too...
would cover, hide and diminish

new generations
know not this nakedness,
still they fight to liberate
the fire born within and
started by tearing off
the clothes draped on our frames
undressing our minds,
unpacking the baggage
carried in chests,
with no treasures in them,
we purged the debris
and are finally...
light enough to fly
to rise up
skin covered in scars

54

woman
an invaluable
masterpiece uncloaked

Transformation

i wonder if caterpillars
fear their evolution
the same way
we do
it's one thing to know
there's greatness
inside,
another to fearlessly
fold into yourself
grow wings
and fly

<u>*Cactus*</u>

caught between
hell and a desert
i mirrored the cactus

pulled life from the
once infertile soil
sprouted spines
became an oasis

you will find a way
to survive
when you have
no choice

<u>Constellations</u>

she was as
unexplored
as a distant galaxy,
trace her scars
and you will find
hidden
c
o
n   S
t   e
ll
a
T
i
on
S

from all the pain
she hid with no consolation

Aura

she was magic
with eyes that
whispered an ancient
language

she was an old soul
with wisdom from
generations

her smile was
illuminating
her aura
was aurora

Nostalgia

i wish i could relax into
remembrance
where only sweet remnants
of our history reside,

i would grab hold
of our fondest moments,
press them against
my chest until they left
a permanent imprint

to have as a keepsake
when i return to reality,
when illusions erase
i long for you
only in my memories

Angel

i still imagine
your angelic face
with eyes that sparkle
in the light

sometimes…
i look up at the sky,
hoping to catch
a glimpse
of your spirit
when the sunlight
breaks through
the clouds

my darling I always knew you would shine

<u>*Grace*</u>

i'm a glimpse of sunshine
during a downpour.
i'm every color of the rainbow.
the reminder there's
always an end
to the storm.

-the meaning of Jayna

<u>*Estranged*</u>

it's strange.
i find myself missing you,
time makes it so easy for me
to forget, sometimes
i really can't
stand you

Blame

i blamed you
for never loving me
when really you tried,
my expectations were unrealistic
i was searching for a love
that only comes from inside

<u>Standard</u>

how could i ever have
found the love of my life
when i had yet to
discover my own?
i let another set the bar
no wonder it was too low.

FULL MOON

illuminated shadows reminded her she was always whole
*****

Someone to Love You

you know that overwhelming
need to love someone else…
maybe it's time
you stop giving it away
and start with yourself

Afro

when your very
existence
is considered
an act of defiance
you have no choice but to
stand up and stand out

Unappreciated

just because i've been
routinely disrespected
doesn't mean i deserve to be.
doesn't mean i'm not special.
i'm a well swallowed by an ocean
i'm what life looks like
when it's taken for granted

time is present

<u>*10 lessons every black girl must unlearn about her hair:*</u>

1. your hair is something that must be fixed
2. you must hide it after it's wet
3. you must "sleep pretty" before special events
4. an afro isn't professional
5. neither are braids, colored hair or extra-long weaves
6. relaxers are your friends
7. there's a such thing as "good hair"
8. it belongs to those with texture 3c or better
9. women with natural hair are intimidating
10. it's just hair— there's no need for these lessons

Caro

she was once trapped
in boxes—placed in boxes
labeled and closed
without
her permission

she winced

whenever i reached
to embrace her,
touching me felt too
much like her small
frame being smothered
by...
more boxes

instead of two hands
she saw
ten more bars,
that would serve to
close her in.

she feared,
as i squeezed
she would have to
once again...
struggle to breathe
that claustrophobia
would kick in,
and instead of
warming
she would
freeze

like she did in

those boxes—
where sunshine
couldn't get in,
where her voice
couldn't get out

she didn't want to
be cold,
but she adapted.
and her defense created
nothing but doubt.

my hugs weren't scary,
but they were triggering

she saw me and wondered,
if i could see her,
or if she was trapped
in a cage lined with
two-way mirrors.
afraid to confirm whether
the boxes
were really gone

she wasn't afraid
of affection.

she winced

when i hugged her,
but the point is
she hugged me back.

*for my sister-friend who taught me boxes and borders, just like arms are meant to
be opened.*

Don't Call My Kettle Black

i've saw a lot of pots
with their true colors burnt off
calling the kettle names
because she mostly burns
at the base
hidden from plain sight
but when it's tea-time
boy does she holler
and the pots look on without
empathy because
they suffer silently
and no one ever comes
to their aid

-colorism divides us

Heartbeat

i wish i could glue
your hand to my chest,
so you could be reminded of
how a heart beats when it adores you.

because you seem to forget.

that your body says,
"i love you"
every time you take a breath.

Seed

from the earth i came, to the earth i return
i thought this was for death,
but this was for growth
i see myself as i will be,
but lord knows that is confusing to me
as i lay here in this soil, but a seed

when the dirt settled over me
its weight pressed down hard on my chest
i was admittedly uncomfortable and i felt
completely alone
surrounded by darkness

i was the only light that shined
and i finally understood why God
would bury me

so that i could learn from the earth
how to photosynthesize.
what's in me is light, and these storms, and this dirt
provide everything i need to survive,
if i can learn to appreciate myself in this tiny season
then i will be rooted in love
and this little seed
will finally grow enough to break ground.
ashes to ashes seed to sprout
i thought i was buried,
but i was planted

Artichoke heart

he asked me
"why i'm so closed off?"
said he wanted to explore
the deepest parts of me.
i knew he had no idea
what his statement meant,
so i offered him
a naked banana
and an orange
stripped of its garments.

he looked confused.
i had given him access
to a never ending
abyss of treasures
still he gazed at me... longing

i sighed,
until you can recognize
the beauty in a naked soul.
one peeled of its covering,
offering nothing
but its inner contents
you can never
appreciate my depth
as a parting gift. i handed him a note that read:

"Everyone isn't meant to feast on artichoke hearts. That is why their shells are so hard.

I am (spoken word)

i am
is scary.
the words that follow after are so defining.
i am
is soul defining—i am art.
it flows from my mouth and hands
i am poetry in motion.
inspiration
strong black woman.
ugh—description
intelligent.
ascription to society's normative illusions
who are you?
compassion—heart bleeding
for everything living and dying.
i'm big and tired of feeling small.
the package isn't
revealing of its content.
rip the façade away.
i'm a free spirit,
so i can't be defined.
and yet when you ask me,
describe your character
i default to this pre-packaged answer,
but its time out for verbatim,
time out for decorum,
and time out for playing like
my depth is safe to descend to
free diving
i'm well beneath the surface.
a well beneath the surface.

you will miss me when your water's gone.
you will miss me if you're not involved.
i am...
spectacular if you let me be
i am...
spectacular if i let me be

Luna

when he told me
i was his
world
i knew he was
the moon
that would stabilize
my tides

#1

you
deserve to be
the number one priority
in someone's life.
you owe it to yourself
to be that
one.

Rain on Me

where i'm from
the skies weep often,
and i have always found
comfort in it.

for the times i lie in bed
on tear stained pillows,
my sobs drowned out
by the beat of mother earth's drum circles

i find comfort
in knowing i'm not the only one who cries.

i find peace
in knowing stormy nights bring new life.

i find solace in knowing
my tears sometimes do the same for me.

that there is a God who sees fit
to rain on me, even when
hell is reigning on earth

-*dear Seattle*

<u>*Self-care*</u>

in you i learned
i can be confident
in my nakedness

making love to myself

Exhale

today
i gave myself permission
to *inhale*.
to take compassionate breathes
that would nourish my soul,
to swallow the light
that would undoubtedly ignite
the flammable particles built-up in my chest.
as i *breathed* in…
i imagined.
god's hand gently clutching my heart
breathing was necessary for life,
so i questioned how
i could not be doing it right

inhale peace.
exhale pain.
this feels different than just *breathing*.
this was living.
deep breath in—savor the feeling
exhale again—this time less resistance
there i was
breathing and living.
and all along i just had
to give myself permission.

<u>Magnetic</u>

walking barefoot
in the sand
i sunk into the earth
she charged me
magnetically,
and everything
i needed became
mine

Free Spirit

loving me demands
the expectation of
evolution and
discovery,
there is no one way
on the path
to me

7 Years

i can't stand watching you
struggle to love yourself

it feels too much like gazing
at an old mirror
from the perspective of my old self
after i already embraced the penalty—
seven years of bad luck
for every mirror i tore up
for every glass i shattered
for every shard i then picked up, and scattered
just to avoid looking
at a reflection that never mattered

forty-nine.
there were seven mirrors
seven times—i couldn't face myself
seven times i couldn't see past images
burned into my memory
images that did not look like me.

i can't stand watching you hate yourself

so seven more years
will be my penalty,
for taking a sledge hammer
to the corners of your face
as you sit here
reflecting.

i'm up to fifty-six now
willingly, i signed up to suffer
another seven years
of a superstitious fate
if it meant you would

stop projecting self-hate
that you would stop reflecting the pain
i broke those mirrors to get away from,
and i would do life to shatter every
unsolicited commentary
that told you,
you weren't good enough.

i've already sentenced myself
to a lifetime of shattering
mirrors and glass,
and all the misfortunes
that come along with it.
if you could just do me this solid.
and walk around
like you finally see yourself,
like you don't ever need
to see another mirror
to be a reflection of light,
like you realize it is always
worthwhile to lose an image
if you gain life
if you gain life
if you gain life,
i will live a lifetime of misfortune
and, i promise you it is worth it

-for everyone who has hidden from their reflection

Rich Soil- (spoken word)

i'm the type of person that gets uncomfortable with permanent decisions.
not because i can't stand by them, in the moment
i mean what i say and i say what i mean,
but life is a journey, so every interaction brings new meaning.
if you're comfortable with being comfortable
then i have to advise you not to plant your seed in my soil.
i'm the foundation that made a rose bloom from concrete
i promise to produce something beautiful,
but i can't promise the cultivation period will always be.
at least by your standards, of comfort and stability.
emphatically, i am keen to nurture, and intent on growth,
but the only thing i do consistently is evolve.
my heart wants to love you,
i just worry that my love won't be enough for you,
and your love won't be willing to adapt with me.
i've never been static, so our electricity is shocking to me.
before you, anchored to one i had never been for long.
lovers they are drawn to my spontaneity,
and i have grown accustomed to the realities that come with change.
the first is that some of the best interactions are short lived.
i've fallen in love with many souls,
tied myself to friendships that never hold.
i'm addicted to falling, so at some point i have to let go,
and yet you're proposing forever—an eternity.
and i'm just wondering if you know that i transform?
that in loving me you will never find a cultivated garden of stability.
do you know that planting your heart in my hands means you're okay with those
terrifying falling dreams,
and crashing into pillows where both of our heads lay?
waking to realize you're holding an imploding bomb in your arms.

do you know i don't boast to be a gardener with a green thumb?
but rather a painter with a different color dripping from each
that i smear on a canvas and watch as blue and red become
one bomb ass shade of purple.

i can't predict who i'll be in a year or three.
i hope it's chasing waves as they recede from the shores.
hearts on sleeves is uncomfortable,
but i'm uncomfortable being comfortable.
do you know what a rush it is
not to calculate ever single aspect of every single day?
to never worry about being late?
do you know what it's like to be free?
and never question why everyone is so different from me?
do you know that my love is pure?
that no matter our differences my commitment to you is sure.
do you know that everything about me ensures that in this lifetime,
you will love many versions of one woman?
that every phase i go through will challenge you?
do you know what it's like to love a woman that loves the way i do?
and are you willing to let a woman like me love you?

H2O

i fell into her. discovered she was
water,
in her i am weightless.

Sorry

she wasn't a box to be checked.
she couldn't be reduced to mandatory time spent.
i promised to learn how to love her.
i promised that i'd learn prioritization.
that she was at the top of the list.

but i was lying.
i did choose her.
i did want her.

but somewhere in all that choosing
i must've lost hold of why,
and that was the moment my yes to her became a lie.
i thought my progress meant
i was done with this test,
but i stepped into another
hidden trap.

again i promised to choose her first.
and i apologized profusely,
for failing to do so previously.
for putting her after

anxiety
stress
and worry

i'm so sorry baby.
self-care is a journey,
and even with a map
sometimes i get lost.
sometimes i forget
you are most important of all

-Dear A'Janee

Forgiveness

i wondered.
why
i couldn't seem to escape you?
why
i couldn't stop reliving
the trauma and being enraged?
i wondered.
why
i was victimized,
and yet i
felt trapped in a cage?
i wondered.
if i had yet again
been party to my own pain?
i couldn't risk forgiveness.
i didn't want to forget,
but if setting you free
is the key
to my freedom
then i'll do it.

Love's Current

like the ocean's tides
sometimes i run away to get lost in myself
in the great expanse
i am still— until i'm not
thank God you're malleable
thank God you let me go

you know i will always return to my sacred shore

you are the sand that takes
the shape of whatever form i'm in
you are the beach that allows
the rest of the world to take photos and caption
you are the earth beneath the moon
that draws me to my ends

you and i are as opposite as dessert and sea,
and yet we don't exist separately
you push i pull— i pull you push.

contrary to opinion
we are perfect in love
you and i don't match up
and yet, you and i without one another
would be so messed up,
so let's not mess this up
thinking we can't be perfectly imperfect.
for that matter
let's not mess this up thinking.

i know the ocean doesn't wonder why it's drawn to the shore.
let's not wonder why we're together anymore.
let's be so beautifully ourselves
that others find peace in our union

let's just be so in love

that i crash into you in every way
let's let our bodies touching be
the most anticipated reunion of every day

<u>Unravel</u>

unravel me…
like my mind is dressed in fabrics you can't wait to rip off.
like my thoughts are the body
you've been waiting and lusting to touch.
unravel me…
like i'm a tangled ball of yarn,
and you're the adoring feline.

unravel me…

like i'm the toughest puzzle to crack.
unravel me until my once bent and crushed back
straightens enough for me to remember,
i'm not stuck in an infinite circular trap.
i want to run away from you,
and know that by creating distance
i'm still guaranteed to end up back in your hands.

unravel…
i mean unpack me
like you're unloading a childhood chest,
and you take pleasure in the nostalgia
of every single piece.
even though we all know there is no blemish free history.
and there's no blemish in her story
that you can't sit with.
can you… go with me
down memory lane, and not get shook and walk away
i mean we're not talking child's play
i'm asking if I bear my truth on these two shoulders
will you then treat me like Quasimodo,
and gawk at my hump back,
or can i unravel sometimes and your loyalty remain in-tact,
or do i have to keep carrying this ball
of pinned up emotion

will i always feel the need to internalize my pain
so much, that i forget it's there
until some fool hits a trigger
and i unravel just enough to convince you
that i'm too messed up.
i'm asking this not expecting an answer and yet,
i'll keep asking these questions
until... i get the right answer.
until...i trust myself enough to give way to vulnerability,
so that i can be a work of art
instead of piles of supplies with no idea of how to start.
can i give myself permission to fall apart

unravel me...
like only you can,
so you can stop taking this baggage into every relationship.
woman...
can you please take the time to unravel on your own,
so that the next time someone tries to love you,
you already love yourself most.
so that if they ever go to leave
they will leave the best of
what you have to offer,
and that can only mean
they were never enough from the start.
unravel now, so you don't have to later.
unravel now, so you know you aren't broken

i know he said you're broken
and maybe you are

but unravel now,
so you realize
you're never broken beyond repair

Keep Turning

when it feels like your
whole world stops revolving
remember there's a
whole universe still turning

MOON PHASES

she can't stop turning. she is the moon, and life is its cycles
***

Testimony
***

Testimony enables reflection and introspection in an age where ignorance is often louder than reason. The opportunity to share personal feelings, stories and experiences offers a less traveled path to healing. In sharing we lift the cumbersome weight of isolation and discover that one of the greatest strengths we possess lies in the telling of our stories.

***

Join the #rockyourtruth movement
now!

Follow Jayna A'janee Smith on
Instagram & Twitter:
@ajanee_poetics

Be sure to go to www. ajaneepoetics.com
To shop healing jewelry, canvas prints, t-shirts and much more